Let the Dead

Let the Dead

Dylan Brennan

BANSHEE
PRESS

First published 2023 by Banshee Press
www.bansheelit.com

A CIP record for this title is available from the British Library.

Grateful acknowledgement is made to Trevor Joyce for permission to
reproduce material from *The Poems of Sweeny Peregrine* (New Writers'
Press), © 1976 Trevor Joyce; and to Mondadori Libri S.p.A. for permission to reproduce material from *Vita d'un uomo. Tutte le poesie*, by
Giuseppe Ungaretti. © 1969 Arnoldo Mondadori Editore S.p.A., Milano
© 2016 Mondadori Libri S.p.A., Milano

Banshee Press gratefully acknowledges
the financial assistance of the Arts Council.

ISBN: 978-1-8383126-9-5

Set in Palatino by Eimear Ryan
Cover design by Anna Morrison
Printed in Ireland by Walsh Colour Print

For my family & friends

Contents

In the cemetery, all the vultures began to circle, and the sky filled with birds.

—Graciela Iturbide

La morte
si sconta
vivendo
—Giuseppe Ungaretti

Let the Dead

And What Is My Heart

and a woman said:
my breasts are milkless
      my eyes are damp
      my skeleton is frail it rattles
and what I want is this:
      I want you to kill me
      to kill me now instead
and another woman said:
      what am I without my child
      and what is my heart
      from this day till the last
      a cold clot of blood

Bog Cotton

Only hours before
the spotting began
we took a walk in the sun and bluster
along the northernmost part
of our island country
and saw the only clouds
were the ankle-high tufts
that marked out for us
like a warning
the softest turf
—common cottonsedge
or bog cotton—
I picked some
and so disrupted / destroyed
anemophilous potential
on that windiest hillbrow

Days later now
on the other side
of the Atlantic
in our tiny apartment
on what were once the shores
of a lake island
the dried flowers spill out
from my wallet
as I look for a phone number
I hold a perianth up
to the morning light
and drink hot coffee
while you sleep

I place the fragile whiteness
on a windowsill saucer
by the cacti and succulents
to be blown out:
carried when the rains come

Kingfisher Haibun

My kingfisher died. I couldn't bear to see him rot. So, I followed the wisdom of the day and kept him dry, placed him in a box. I stuffed the box into my wardrobe. It sat there for years behind grey banks of old jeans with turned-up hems where dust, soil, shards of twigs accumulated. You see, if you keep the corpse of a kingfisher in a dry condition it will never decay. If placed in a wardrobe among garments the halcyon bird will ward off moths and preserve your clothes with its pleasant odour. I thought often of adorning his resting place with hydrangea petals or a sprig of eyebright but was worried about moisture and so left his box as it had always been, a drab brown geometry. I would sometimes forget he was there until catching a whiff of that fragrance from the corner like a wicker basket of springtime blossoms from the riverbank, a meandering nosegay that could reach as far as the breakfast table and mingle with the steam from my coffee. I would take him out to show visitors who marvelled at his colours: the front plumage like the setting sun on a rusting trawler and a turquoise glimmer of sea.

All this.
All this to what end.

When he was alive he would land on my wrist and eat the aquatic insects I gathered for him. He once even let me tighten my fingers around his breast to feel the soft mania of his beating heart and we existed together, so very close to the fresh water. Now he is cold and not living and I am down here with a tiny raft I've fashioned from discarded fish bones, twine and dental floss. I place him on the bone-craft and kiss him goodbye, push him away, launch his last journey. The raft takes on water. The process of disintegration has already begun. I stand here with cold circles around my ankles.

a clump of blue feathers
darkens then sinks—my hand
cups a ripple

After an Ultrasound

I find myself down the back field
surveying the flora at my toes

beige and purple clover blossoms
and violet heal-alls or woundwort

among the green asterisks of dandelion
and near the white flecks of yarrow

a fragile trefoil I identify later
(reverse image search on my phone)

and more familiar yellows of buttercups
and daisy hearts and knocking gently

against my shins the stooping
black heads of the ribwort plantain

(a wildflower once used to bring
back the dead)   and I think of how

as children   we just called it all grass

Four Attempts at Making a Human

(not) after Popol Vuh

i.

this is what happened
we made a small person out of mud
& placed it down there on the table
just like the gods (heart of sky)
we rolled up our sleeves (heart of sea)
to get our hands dirty
in the stuff of life
but something went wrong
its neck wouldn't turn
it just stared up at us
a tiny face with no understanding
a barely pulsating thing
(it couldn't think)
like an overcooked vegetable
(it couldn't worship)
a sort of primal
gurgle of lamentation
as it dissolved in hot droplets
into nothing

ii.

There's an old joke about the car made out of wood: wooden engine and dashboard, wooden wheels, the only problem—it wooden start. Something similar here. You see, we are chiselled, framed and shaped in the mouths of our peers, remembered by tongue. And so we did it again. We made a little person, a wooden effigy, and gave it some words. She crawled briefly before stopping, spoke eloquently until her face dried up into a kind of expressionless, desiccated mask. Her arms and legs turned stiff, an unresponsive little body, rigid and cold. No blood flowed within, no oil or sweat. We remembered stories of similar cases, effigy corpses left to be devoured, mouths and faces ruined and crushed, twig-bones snapped, ground up for the dogs, and so we kissed her goodbye and submerged the crumbling husk in an organic and fragrant resin before burning. We inhaled the smoke, smeared the ashes on our arms and chests as the whole earth darkened in a thick black rain. And that was that. To remind me of our little wood-girl experiment, I keep a single splinter ingrained, a speck I carry with me in the palm of my hand.

iii.

ah, my darling wife, we've never been gods
can't make corn into anything but food
and so it took us a fourth attempt (no, I'll not
mention the third) for the expected shock:
a flush of rose water in the middle of breakfast

we wove our wildflowers into a son: a filigree
of bog cotton, mouse-ear, mayweed, bedstraw,
bittercress dampened with sea foam, eyebright
and yarrow strengthened with dried strips
of henequen   and he was born and lived and grew

After the Storm

Greens, lilacs, greys: a soft dampness of aftermath. You are an old woman in a painting, an experiment in style from the formative years. You move through dawn, a littoral zone. The coastal land a scab that rocks gently against salt water, perpetual dissolve. Jagged limbus of a bitten fruit. The best part just beneath the apple skin. Always towards the boat wreck. Fleshy silver with metallic glints then gutted, disemboweled at night by storms. Wooden ribcage whistling and beckoning. Time. All that remains. Canvas, bacteria, fire. The fibres of a body. With your mourning clothes and inclined beetle-gait you are easily read. From left to right in the Western tradition, slowly you walk in the direction of words.

Botany

Cuetlaxóchitl: How could I not think of the 'flower that withers' and its heavy red petals you moistened this morning with a lukewarm spray, the same petals that, pre-conquest, were dried to an infusion to increase breast-milk production, organized triangles planted down the boulevard now like an artery to Chapultepec, the failing lungs of our megalopolis. For some, the remembrance of slaughtered warriors; for others, a broken little heart wailed into existence. Or a sign of the Christ cut from the roadside and sent to a slave owner's greenhouse in South Carolina. Hard to cultivate in the high lake valley, caravans from the south at year's end carried to the emperor and distributed to temples, the scarlet return of a low sun to ensure new life, continued light. This solstice it's just the two, no, three of us: the tiny boy (unwithered) punches softly in your belly.

Móin: I ran along the Moat Road that divides Dublin from Wicklow as the sun felt as cold and silver as the pooled bog water in which it was reflected. I chanced upon three apiaries nestled in a damp geometric hollow of turf cut to be burned in winter. I saw no bees. The only sound my heavy breathing in the sphagnum freshness. A satellite tracked my run. I stepped from the path to crouch and touch some heather when my feet sank down through sodden black fibres. With legs darkened to the knees I got back to the car where my father waited with a hot flask of tea. The next time running was back in the Alameda with my shoes still partially caked in bogland detritus. With little warning, the last downpour of the year came upon me in heavy glass sheets, flushing the Irish sediment out into the park. I watched it dissolve in runnels of rainwater.

Alameda: The presence of the virus means the Alameda (built on swampland and named for the poplars that have since been replaced) is blocked off with metallic barricades, allowing the squirrels and grackles to wander the interior unmolested, as human beings have been requested to no longer gather. Nevertheless, at the southern end, opposite the Palace of Fine Arts, a group of women remain camped. They sell handmade trinkets under posters and photographs of the recently disappeared and weave into the morning a grief so acute it clutches still to a hope: that the state will somehow bring back the dead. At the north-eastern corner of the rectangle the last jacaranda blossom hangs on. Planted in the thirties, suggested by Matsumoto as a more resilient alternative to cherry trees, they enliven the centre every spring. They leave normally with the summer torrents that blow the bruised-to-black petals out into the streets to clog drains with polystyrene scraps and discarded half-limes that turn the city back into its former self: a chaotic assemblage of plazas and canals. Purple florets waver on a branch—they might just make it to New Year's.

Anacahuita

the anacahuita came
to blossom while we waited

to leave hospital and now greets
our arrival back home   how sweet

to see those milk cups
blur on the horizon   white freckling

the land as far as the eye can focus
but no   everywhere we look

wildflowers give way
to encroaching rectangles

my son you see   this is what they do
from García to Monterrey

they're flooding
the plains with concrete

how long this will last
is anyone's guess

so for now   just breathe
this citric welcome

I'll show you pictures
when you're older

17

The Dead

tender failure in a remote
corner of a room

scattered patches
of pale red

What the Swan Can Teach Us

we must be
like the swan

& exhibit
in our own

funeral
melodies

a serene
contempt

for loss
of life

Julio César Mondragón

an accordion player dribbling drunk
on a street in Chilpancingo—green twinkles
of damiana-infused mezcal

seventeen years from now
electric pink *quinceañera* dresses
scrunching in a mist of sweet perfume

a fearless boy contorting from La Quebrada
before smashing into seawater

*

scooped or gouged from their sockets
they took his eyes away

and the things he'd seen
the things he might have seen

Christmas, Oaxaca

Noche de Rábanos. A giant flea nursing a bottle of mezcal, a bug-eyed parrot swaying in the evening, a pastoral tableau, an abundance of nativity scenes. We duck in through a gap in the railings to get to the interior where something vile awaits us amid the posters and placards—his perfect teeth surrounded by this crimson mess of exposed flesh. We didn't ask to see this and we move away, drifting through choppy rivers of brass bands that march through the streets, each trying to drown the other. Trucks with children dressed as angels and shepherds followed by dancing girls with magnificent layered skirts and men holding bamboo-framed giants with papier mâché heads. All dance and twirl, multi-coloured dervishes enraptured in their shared dreams. Earlier I saw a boy play a sousaphone he'd fashioned from plastic water bottles, begging for cash. I look for him now but, of course, he doesn't feature. This event is important—these instruments impeccable. Metallic and polished, they twinkle in the night. Fireworks exploding and a rain of sulphur and primary colours bathes us all in its pungent glow. Children everywhere, pregnant girls everywhere and the blank stares of the *normalistas* in the background—all is magnified, all there is to be gobbled up like fried grasshoppers, life and death in every blink. Prawn bisque with roasted almonds, piping hot turkey with a fruits-of-the-forest sauce, stuffing infused with apricot purée, pears soaked in aniseed and red wine with cinnamon ice cream. The noise of the fireworks and parading *mojigangas* diminishes slowly. After coffee a little girl plays an accordion on the corner and I give her some coins. Back to bed through the *zócalo*, a shrine of purple candles and lights in the shape of '43'. A text message from the local news service tells us Peña Nieto, the charm president, the haircut president, wishes all a happy Christmas, a peaceful Christmas and an end to violence. A poster picture of that boy with a young lady and a baby in his arms and I wonder if, in their dreams and memories, that smile will return to them or if they'll be faced with an abomination, red and despicable. On the shores of obsidian sleep I wonder what they did with his eyes and I close my own.

Cocoon

[...] the corpse, the most sickening of wastes, is a border that has encroached upon everything.

—Julia Kristeva

i. city (resignation)

a film forms as my coffee cools
—the border solidifies
it wrinkles, ripples in the breeze
from a doorway to the street
I dip my metal spoon
into the glass, lightly, so as
not to pierce, so that it pulls
in its skirts from the rim   see it
hang from the convex as it's raised to my lips
—see the flayed skin on the chapel wall

coriander, lime & onions
a warm muscle in my mouth
vapours from a bovine lowing
liquefy on my moustache
a modest scent of corn steam
makes itself known to my nostrils
damp cud under a soft moon
circles, dimples, slowly chewed
texture of tongue meat sporadically toughens
valves that are sliced were blue before cooked

the blood in your body settles
in accordance with the laws
of gravity, perhaps pooling
in your cold toes & ankles
which I'll cover up
with woollen socks like brown rabbits
skin chilled like plucked gooseflesh
rigidity in the muscles
stubborn to the grave with a sunken-eyed stare
I'll sit by your side—you won't be there

ii. cloud forest (cleansing)

fluttering mass of eyes & stripes
thickening the cloud forest
we see Mexican Silverspots
Zebra Longwings splashing light
across these ferny landways
(the Polyphemus Moths blinking
at the Anna's Eighty-Eights)
we give to all its proper name
as rainwater pools in the
prints of a black bear

more green upon greens that darken
under rainfall, dinosaurs
eat & trample upon species
unvaried across aeons
I run my fingers over
chlorophyll fronds & fiddleheads
as anvil droplets turn to
drizzle   mist   memory
tendrils unfurl with a relative quickness
—energy stored until solar death

resilient threads of yellow flesh
weaved across a biscuit floor
touchable steam wafting moonwards
the cloud forest moistening
our oxygen   the stars
water the black void above us

we'll fatten ourselves tonight
from the soils a perfect sweetness
begs to be tempered by tepid coffee
foliage envelops us, insects scream

iii. semi-desert (introspection)

dry branches in the dust-winds
fingernails can slit the skin
to drench the desert in latex
oxygen turns it to gore
sangre de grado, sangre de drago
—dragon or menstrual plasma
depending on where you're from
these branches we twist and snap
    as we walk on
hot stones in the night

cruel bronze rips away genitals
killers wash their feet & hands
return quickly to their masters
(it's a daily occurrence
you're with them or against them)
cartilage, organs, valves & skin
—sticky dinner for house dogs
home for good, disembodied tongues
the relentless yammer the
sounds that still rock us to sleep at night

delicate anthers shy
away from breath & nostrils
then are discarded
we cut fruit with credit cards
slip its chunks into segments
of winter-ripened mandarins

embryonic cactus
      cosmic alkaloids
the ambers of a bleeding sunscape
prepare us for what is yet to come

iv. void (lamentation)

clean air & baby Jesus
in the clouds, you'll be sitting
up in no time drinking
sugary cups of milky
tea   you're not dying
on the roadside
you're a supernova sweetpea
just close your eyes to see
a sparkly blackness in the curvatures of space
—a wonderverse, a handful of dust

either it's this   integrated
thought   synergy   more than the
sum of the neurons   the network
   the two plus two that equals
five   with the death of the brain
it leaves you forever   or it's
something else   computer code at
the void's edge   the face of a god
yawning over the waters   axons   silence
   synaptic gaps   chaos   post-flesh

deities gasp for attention
unwitnessed quantum vacuum
at the outset there was nothing
m'illumino d'immenso
ripples ripple eternal
fiat lux—ending to begin

a balloon pop in the void
dark matter stretching out forever
decimation stardust creeps under doorways
& nothing has still   not been observed

v. darkroom (butchery)

facial tendons young & twitching
black blood gurgles
& the camera hand trembles
what is this that you're watching
what   in this click-share swirl
so painlessly it brings you
so numb so long so young so
dark her hair that sticks to her face
the need to perceive all the things of this earth
have stained you   have buried you alive

disturbed by street dogs
diagonal man across path
out here   windswept graveyard
a turn-the-corner surprise
—still his jeans upon his legs
the face is gone, skull exposes
a mouthful of bleached white teeth
for a chiaroscuro effect
focus & shoot   questions are for your darkroom
—buy a silver fish in the market

eventually his remains
will collapse in a humid
moving mess upon unhallowed
grounds with no dried fruits or herbs
to be burned within nose-reach
the writs yanked from grieving sisters

the rituals disallowed
to be pecked at & gnawed upon
by time & the indifference of fauna
there is no is—clepsydra, drip on

vi. village (definition)

looking not unlike bisected
brains (imagine their skulls
left spinning slowly
on the shifting sands
of the glassy ocean)—coral, shells
& polished stones held once
in place by sea-mortar
upon this reassigned land
first colonial house crumbles
gently strangled for centuries

caramel sun power outage
languid collapse of cardboard
boxes of delivered ice cream
copper bells clank the hours
on decayed bone   the feathers
of crows harden, yellow pink brown
reverberating croaks through
the narrow streets   sticky trickles
of Neapolitan sweet milk & our lips
not the only down kissing the stone

it's the beginning of death—a
kind of mummification
silver nitrate, a flat jar of
amber   so long as eyes can
see, portraits deceive—baby
in the open white box, puffy

33

ankles—father, cowboy hat
removed, coffin carried upon
the flat of his cranium   rigid little
thing—fingernails the size of drizzle

vii. home (grief)

you—moving in ever-widening
& quickening ellipses
around my core—increasingly
watery, blurred, translucent
memory threads narrative
quid sum miser tunc dicturus
a day without yesterday
ingemisco tamquam reus
our multiverse particles still zoetic
—annihilation is a falsehood

I rub your back while your insides
contract & evacuate
to leave your body & this house
death is taking his sweet time
slowly trickling the remnants
of hope of newness of young blood
the unviable
our speciality it seems
'I can never again go through this'
no fear, no fear, a nation of two

mornings spent under shit-splatter
there are squares & rectangles
—black & white spaces out here where
people still live—damp flat land
constructed upon rubbish
squawks & warbles weave the skyline

35

I dust myself in birdseed
lie down, spreadeagled, mouth opened
organic cold matter moistens my t-shirt
I flinch awake & the sky scatters

Stories Made Flesh

At the Sunday food market in San Rafael the vendor calls it *yaca*. It tastes like soursop, like a peach, like mango and something else. Plump petals of yellow flesh round a smooth stone. A thin living film on hard surface, toughened embryonic sac. Breadfruit and jackfruit are often confused. They are related. They look similar from the outside. The white meat of the breadfruit could cure world hunger but its yellow cousin tastes so much better.

Now in the market there are things I avoid. For example, I can't look at those soft little heaps, light green under drizzle, the fava beans speckled with diced onions and chillies. Not since you held our own little fava in front of me. And all that blood. All of it now. Bathroom window cracked open. The brief wisp of steam from cupped hands, dissipation of organic. Dissipation of a self.

A few months ago a rat crawled under our front door, escaping from a downpour and blocked drains. It tore apart bags of flour and rice while we slept. On a Friday night we drank wine and stayed up late to catch it. An almond in peanut butter, the sound of a snapped neck and very little blood. When I picked it up, black bag round my hand, it felt so much heavier than it should. I am terrified of rats. You said I should hold it by its tail—I don't know why.

*

Christopher Columbus was told by the Taíno people of Hispaniola that the gold and precious rocks he searched for could be found on a smaller, nearby island. He searched for this place to no avail. A map he drew contains a hole in the parchment. It is believed that this absence represents the apocryphal island of material riches. Centuries later an artist sails out to find nothing but seawater and a small piece of driftwood. He gathers a hundred litres of the sea and, as he evaporates the liquid slowly, a white crystal forms. Coaxing the material from the patently illusory, the imagined, invented islet is conjured from the waters, is willed into existence. A tangible phantom and a crystallized anchorage. Now it's on the floor in front of me, like a dream or the words of a story made flesh. I long to pick it up, taste that salt on my tongue. My arms are cold, a frozen ink trudges through my insides.

*

are there rats
down there
do they eat
fleshy lumps

The gurgle of water finding its level, the darkness that enters seeps through the wounds. I've thought often of the hole we could have dug. For a place you can point at. One hollow for another. To a boxed-off kind of grief. But things in the ground have a tendency to grow.

he's a milk-azure marble under moonlight

she's a shard of smashed obsidian

they're the night falling out all around us

The Dead

silver glimmering
down in his heart

the silence in
a man's throat

Hy Brasil

as far as I can tell
the history of this settlement

is the history of them all:
men and women

huddling together
at the cold edge of a void

we know of ancestors
though they wrote nothing down:

shell middens, fish traps
and lithic debris

have been found upon
the offshore islets

a primal meal: a bubbling
of mussels boiling in seawater

oysters and whelks sucked raw
with the salts of a lacerated knuckle

our outcrop is spared
the bitter poison of the yews

aquatic birds squawk down
on us from their crags

(when our feet get longer
we will hunt them with ease)

this is a friable country
of uneven surfaces

with standing waters
on the tops of our mountains

(you thought I'd speak of honey
milk and meadows)

our wide estuary drinks
deeply from the foam

brackish waltz
at the river mouth

a dark freshness
rises to nothing

the further
you travel east

the brighter and clearer
the sky's face

where the river seeps
up through turf

we scavenge for squirms
muddy eels, oily shads

it is impossible
to leave

we have the ocean
alone on the west

Things You Can Do With a Grasshopper

If you decapitate a grasshopper it will sing
for you sweetly for a while before dying.

If you place a grasshopper up to his neck
in the snow he'll stay congealed for a time

until you return to find and decapitate him
then (the dulcet tones all the more delicious

for having waited a full season for that insect
melody). By the warmth of your hands

and breath, you could coax one back to wonder.
You could pluck a handful from our fields

of trampled ice and (when the hop and flutter
of rebirth tickle your fingers) release them

in the meadows of a land where
we've not yet begun to behead.

Of an Island Where Corpses Exposed to the Atmosphere Do Not Suffer Decay

Herzog propped them all
up against a wall and filmed
them slowly one by one. The mummies
of Guanajuato look like they died
screaming but it's just this—the jaws
slacken when we die, our mouths fall open.
We'll all expose our fillings to a lens.
The gales, the salts of the sea
and the ashen sands of the shore
preserve the corpses of our kinsmen.
Look—that man's father and *his* father
recognize themselves among the strewn
bodies of Inis Gluaire—sun-tanned
leatherfaces like shipwrecked Spaniards.
Spectral arcs of colours through the constant
drizzle. Go kneel down upon the damp earth,
we'll join them soonish on the lazy-beds.
On this island there are no black rats.

I Crammed My Mouth

No hope for him this time
night after night faintly and even

two candles at the head
paralysis, fear and worms

endless little black eyes
I crammed my mouth

drew blankets over my head
tried to think but the face

still followed me—he was gone
and I was disturbed to find myself

*

I walked to the sun on tiptoe
end of the dusky light

black cavernous flowers
her skirt was hooked at the back

I groped the stem of her
wine glass before sipping

*

no noise lying still in his coffin
such a beautiful corpse

when all is done
a body can trust

Ghost Brides

Men work hard all their lives and sometimes forget to get married. These unfortunates grow old and die, but must not be buried alone. This would bring bad luck upon their souls. A companion must be found. Bones are required, those of a female. One man thought of buying a woman made of dough to be buried with his brother. Pebbles or fruit pits in the hollows for her eyes, reworked pillowcases for her modesty. But the elders told him of rats as large as human heads and the misfortune brought about by the use of fake women. Only a genuine specimen would do. A girl and her skeleton were found for the burial. Sourced locally through an agency she was fortified by means of metal wiring and rendered more rigid. Though she did not caress or cook for him in life, in death she would cleave to him and obey.

Notes on Black Vultures

I've been reading up on those new world vultures ever since we spotted them through the train window at the edge of Sinaloa. How the lack of a syrinx means they're silent save for an occasional hiss and grunt if disturbed whilst feeding. How their bald heads protect against the infection from trapped remains of decaying flesh under feathers.

> A heavy glide with short bursts of laboured flapping. The white trim on the underside only visible in flight, photogenic against magnesium sky. A flying group of vultures is known as a kettle.

'*Cim cehil* is a stock Maya expression for *drought*'. What it means is this: *when the deer die*. Therefore, an image of an expiring stag, goggle-eyed, tongue lolling, taunted by a god upon the plain— is a way to depict a shortage of water. *Kuch caan chacil* means the rains from a vulture sky. Vulture sky rain is no good for crops. Vulture rain means drought.

> A vulture. Alone. Omen in the rain. A standing glyph.

Roosting on power cables as the sun goes down or on desert trunks caked in dust. A resting collective is not known as a murder or a parliament, the names I would have chosen, but as a venue, a volt or a committee.

> Presiding over a dead suburban cat. Squabbling on the internet beneath impeccable sunshine.

Mostly they feed on carrion but will sometimes descend upon a newborn calf, nipping at its gooey eyeflesh, stunning the emerging creature, picking it apart. The word for black vultures feasting on a newborn is a wake.

> I've seen them on your chest at night.
> Feathers, a scattering of darkness as I reach out to touch.
>
> The word for a group of black vultures that perch on the sleeping body of a loved one is a clench.

The name for the covered area between carriages on a passenger train is a vestibule and there I found you leaning out the window to photograph the movement of clouds across the river, the cacti and eagles. I remembered walking in the field behind the house in Knocklyon, how surprised you were by the sudden retreat of shade. Irish light in summer shifts easily across us like pondwater rippling upon land. I thought of this as a silent kettle ascended to sky from their yucca perches. It cast a fleeting form across your face. A short-lived optogram of flight before dissipating in retina. You looked up from the camera and smiled. A face lighter for the blackness that passed. The word for this is a *fluttering*.

Stoneflower

Away from the acid glow
of sulphur crystals, Yves Klein crumble
of azurite, translucent gypsum
and the glisten of quartz lumps,
nestled in a drab cabinet of fossils
a flower I can never give you.
300 million years ago slowly trapped,
dug up in what is now still Ireland—
actinocrinus stellaris. Strange to say
in encyclopaedias and online archives
I can find next to nothing other than
this: extinct genus of the crinoid,
from the Greek: *krinon-eidos*—form of a lily.

The Dead

soft pyramid
of bone

the babe still
cold in her hand

First Snake in Ireland

must have been as he lay snoring
a grass snake from the pond
a slithering baby into his mouth
down into the darkness
an intestinal warren

must have eaten its way through
last night's dinner a mush of chewed lamb
shallots enzymes of Rhine wine
or an oaty pottage and bolshy ale

lateral moraine of leftovers
squirming belly
of doubling-over quiver-pangs

no burnt offerings
did the trick no leeches did they ever
snakey fissures
the forked tongue
rounding the splenic flexure

*

slight decrease in moan-curses
Isle of Man dissipates in salt-mist
the waves lashed his little wooden boat

the bow cracked land a sharp
ankle-whack on the crag of a rock pool
squashed anemones underfoot
a limpet scrape on his smallest toe

fever overtook him fresh flannels of seawater
his forehead a woman his nose boiled cockles
the steam of an elderflower infusion

he dreamt a giant squid his neck
a stranglehold then awoke shivering in filth

amongst
the texture of grains
he found his fingers wrapped
round the blue corpse of a serpent

the thing that had been his torment

alive and alone he stumbled naked
to marram grasses
to lie down and bathe
in morning's dew and tidespray

his ankle purple swollen and cold

Ireland's Eye

The northern gannets, black-and-white razorbills
damp ferns, creamy speckle of cow parsnip
that unexpected carpet of large daisies
that led us to the summit with our sandwiches
—Lily, my brothers, a friend who'd lost his mother
we ate and passed my hip flask around
single malt whiskey and sun-dried tomatoes
salted on our tongues by easterly seaspray

I take down now from the kitchen shelf
a jar that used to contain mustard and pour
onto the table what I took from that island
what Simon scooped up into an old crisp packet
—microscopic fan shell upon sand and pebbles
and what I think is the vertebra of a fish
taken cold from the Irish Sea and dashed on rocks
—a matte organic little puck that sits on top

I brush it all back into the jar
(the crushed saltiness of motherland)
in the flexion creases of my palm
some traces remain

Glencree

The ferns around the rims
of the fan-shaped cemetery
Photos of the sick, dead or grateful
moulder in the grotto
Mercury ripples
of the twin tarns above
—glacial descendants nestled in moraine

Bag-of-bone ghosts
of St Kevin's Reformatory
still porous by the brick facade
blue knuckles shovelling
snow before breakfast
—escaping to Dublin or exposure
on the Featherbeds

Those Kriegsmarine
and Luftwaffe who fell
anonymous to this island
or washed up purple
on the beaches and civilians
torpedoed by their own countrymen
—denied a life post-Canadian internment

The last river I stood in
—the brief miracle
of a mountain stream
on a ruptured tendon
and the massage
of the larger pebbles
on the tired arch of the foot

Dublin Nocturne

cold cans of cider
under pockmarks of rock
burst capillaries

fur-lined hoods
standing in line
Christmas food parcels

non-perishables
sugar, cereal, tinned fish
in blue plastic bags

you'd get sick of soup
purple lines your face
winter fingers dead

ragged decorations
Apollo House
red and green on gate

Christ of black bile
the mumbled prayers
unsettling mists

saturnine man holds
sway over dirty waters
sinks down into minerals

moon knows not her strength
stars know not their station
blackness swallows all

freckles, gaunt faces
addiction is the problem
please feed my rabbit

your only man
Poolbeg Street
downing an absence

pin cushion sky
and a toothless mouth gumming
at the

rabbit or a man in moonmist, habitual lodger, which came first?
Fresh at sea when the moon also was standing in a corner of
sweet. Lune, waxer, waner, gloamer, gleamer, buttery cueball—
hung above us at the beginning of spacetime so we could count
the days, something peculiar to our universe.

Lullaby

fragment of bone and a molar

ruined calcium cold to touch
bury him in clay even colder

Tamaulipas Amergin

i. A Song of Amergin

I'm the blue land crab lost near the salt marsh
I'm the phantom islet that's appeared on your map
    (poured-out-like-water darkness)
I'm the mangrove that gropes through the delta for soil
    (brackish ripples near the swollen beachwort)
I'm a sick thing forming in your drinking water
I'm your dream of the semi-desert
    (a cold river taken whole in your mouth)
I'm the shaved head of your friend in the pit
I'm a cloth of worms, I'm that addled flesh
    (calligraphy on your chest that moves in the night)
I'm the turkey vulture that circles over thorn scrub
I'm the blackberry blossom that trembles in drizzle
I'm the marrow that's needed to moisten your body
    (the fresh white of an egg)
I'm the green dampness of a fertile valley
    (the rain that's been withheld)
I'm the last living ghost sitting down among ashes
    (if only his thoughts were printed in a book)
I'm the Christmas cactus with its scarlet flecks
I'm a frail enough thing to be broken like a twig
I'm a jawbone thrown on the heap
I'm the silt that separates one nation from another
and the sodden black harvest of a gaunt island

ii. The River Before War

Boys and men from both sides
would bathe in the river before war

stepping on the same sediment
so close they could touch

bobbing and rising lightly
in the swell and pull

of the enemy's ripples
sleeping in their camps

with the river inside them
in their hair

and under fingernails

iii. Why I Cross the River

My waterlogged country
its softened edges
begin to fade from memory

An ink of feathers across
the surface, blackbirds
disguised as bathing women

A hedge before me I long
for an island, a land full of stars
I'm as ruthless as I am poor

At least there'll be music
down there and a softer bed
I'm fragile, damp and in pain

The sweetest thing I imagine:
the defeated face of an enemy
in an open desert country

The mesquite thorn like grief
lodged under the skin
the limitation of horizon

I stir vinegar into my coffee
as an antidote to stupor
I travel to my death in silence

iv. Desertion

edge of life
the sturdy corn is green

(there is no green darker
than a cornfield in the rain)

every dream I have
I crouch to where

a woman is sunk in clay
I'm in want of an amulet

against loneliness
I pray and the body decays

—these mountains
tell the distance

through mist and
foam to desire—

beyond the muscles of the river
is a widespread country

I tour this land in bewilderment
and see my mother as a buzzard

v. Towards a Decision

light fell over
childish eyes

he looked down
to the river

when his sight
cleared a little

held the waning
sunset

to his breast
in fright
(it's so beautiful)

tried to weigh his soul

dusk flickered
upon his shadow
(of course it's beautiful)

'may you never die
till I shoot you!'

godspeed
from gaunt
& spectral
men

vi. What He Currently Desires

a sweet confluence
of waters

to steep
a fevered brain

a light
& silver skiff
to smooth
the wrinkles
of the sea

to attain
my former rank
or die
in the trying

dizzy music
& the blaze
of the dance

honey & hazelnuts
fresh milk & pork

an invitation
to a pillow

a cure
for sorrow

a roof   warmth   & touch

vii. Traitor

a sheaf held together
in the very dark twilight

fearing collapse
he slackened his pace

the right side of his head
had been injured

no warm soil around
exotic feet—cold & white

he turned gleaming eyes
to the grey river

& the reality
his memory told him

a black iron sky
& no one wanted him

viii. *Uisce* in Linares

the first time
Gaeilge

was whispered
on the streets

of Linares
must have been

the morning
they collapsed

in the plaza here
like famine victims

to gulp at
fresh spring water

& earn
that *colorados*

nickname for
their burnt skin

after a battering
from the enemy

just north of
Matamoros

where they first
began to desert

dodging volleys
of musket balls

to be welcomed
by church bells

though some were
not so lucky:

Henry Lamb
& Carl Gross

shot from the bank
& four or five

catholics in broad
daylight

headlocked down
to the river bottom

I remember another
who thrashed about

in that border rush
that's taken so many

how black
& cold & so lonely

ix. La Angostura

steep the ruins
of your body
in the river
like ointment
scratch our names
down there on a rock

x. The Dream Before

web of noise
from a convulsed body

a sombre halo
pale disc of a face

large faint moon
solitary & unique

small eyes below
that seem to meditate

a ravaged brain
(a throat)

a memory of texture
(a tongue)

deep & full
a twilight throbs

in the devil hand   a small gold coin

xi. Outside Monterrey

I crouched
to gawp

at two horses
still eating

sooty grasses
as their entrails

slumped out
into the morning

xii. The Soil

is black as the mush of the blighted spuds
that drove so many westwards
as black as the coffee outside Montemorelos
as cold as the endemic species of Nuevo León that exist out
    there in the darkness:
rare variations of goldenrods and Gordon's bladderpods
sparks of yellow, desert flats, gypsum soils
and the needles of the cacti I can see
because I know they are out there pricking at the vapours
black as the moonless gloom of the battle of Monterrey
the soot on lungs behind cannons at the citadel
unbreathable clouds from the twelve-pound howitzers
grapeshot, sandbags, cobblestones, pickaxes
and the corrugated coughs of the boys with yellow fever
of the chlorophyll voids of gaping mouths
of an entire island abandoned by their god to ingest infected pulp
the biles of their sadness dripping back to the soil
cursing the earth, black as hunger
and the beating of a man till he stops

xiii. Far From Home

Fresh blue petals my   grief is nightblooming

xiv. Mammy / *Nonantzin*

Please mammy when I die
Bury me under the kiln
And when you're baking the bread
You can cry for me there

If a passer-by asks
Missus why all the tears
Say the firewood's still damp
And the smoke hurts your eyes

The Dead

Lily lies
shivering

against
my ribs

Black Honey

As we move away from Ciudad Victoria I imagine how quiet Santa Engracia, off to the west, must feel in the small hours of this dark morning. How lonely and black the abandoned honey. I picture the corpse of that man near the layers of wax, the land still a dumping ground for the Zetas and cops. Entomological architecture is something to be admired. It was only at the end of the last century that a human mathematician confirmed what the bees have always known, that their hexagonal structure of prismatic cells is the most efficient system for storage within a fixed boundary. A while back, some local women asked Lily's uncle for permission to set up their colonies in the orange and mandarin groves. But one morning as the sun crept over from adjacent bean fields, they came across some bodies near the hives. Or just one body, in pieces. The flesh now decomposing, the honey untouched inside the wooden drawers or maybe dripping down upon those remnants of a person. I remember legends I've heard of the mellified Arabian, glad to donate his body to the healing of bones, centuries in the future, consuming only honey until it oozed in a paste from his pores and anus, sold as a rare and expensive remedy across Asia, a fragrant confection for the betterment of others. But this is not some selfless donation. That he's gone back to the land might mean something to his family, if they could only be told. There are things up here that we just can't talk about. We continue driving north-west, out past farmlands under carpets of a statewide cloud cover. We cross the Purificación river under an absence of starlight, the river where I've seen youngsters bathing in summer while their families sell chillies and orange juice through the windows of vehicles. We move quickly on the slick road through mists. Monterrey waits for us at dawn but, for now, the world is just a black wet fur up against us.

Sokushinbutsu

Millet, soybeans and rice are gradually
eliminated from your diet—replaced
by cold berries, nuts, bark shavings
and some tea—an infusion made from the leaves
of the *urushi*, our beloved lacquer tree.
Induced vomiting eliminates fats from
the body as it lines itself with the heat
of an embalming fluid. Dehydrated,
puckered organs begin to shrink,
as your skin turns into poisonous leather,
too vile even for maggots.
Now sit yourself down alone to chant
and ring your bell at regular intervals that lengthen until
the energy fails you, the bell clunks once and drops.
In a hundred days they will check in
on you to see if self-mummification
and sainthood have been achieved or, indeed,
if putrefaction of the corpse has occurred.
If the former, you will be worshipped
as a holy relic. If the latter, you'll be walled
back up. There are other possibilities.
For example, your brother's cadaver
is now a hatchery for geckos.

Striking Worker, Assassinated

i.

Manuel Álvarez Bravo, with his Striking Worker, Assassinated,
has risen to the heights of what Baudelaire has called 'eternal style'
—André Breton

It looks so wet so fresh, the black bile red
spills out across earth, luscious hair
the crops and soil smell of bleeding fingers
searching mothers with broken nails
far from the temples in the steam of the isthmus
a young man, a boy, his head blown out the back
a secular event, predictable and logical
they'll mythologize this, mysticize it
the cultural historians who've never set foot

ii.

Aside from everything I've said, Mexico tends to be the surrealistic place par excellence. I find surrealist Mexico in its topography, its flora, in the dynamism arising from its racial mixture, and in its highest aspirations.

—André Breton

It turns out that the simplest act
of surrealism might be to think
you hear fireworks in the nearby
village to rush upon the aftermath
of a workers' protest and stare
down into the open eyes
of a boy to shoot
his corpse with your camera

iii.

The image is a pure creation of the mind. It cannot be born from a comparison but from a juxtaposition of two more or less distant realities. The more the relationship between the two juxtaposed realities is distant and true, the stronger the image will be—the greater its emotional power and poetic reality.

—Pierre Reverdy

Q: Why did the first patriarch come from the west?
A: The cypress in the orchard.
Q: What is the Buddha?
A: A family of rats in the basement.
Q: What are we doing here?
A: Green scum on a stagnant pond.
Q: Why must one meditate?
A: A snapped-back fingernail ripped from the flesh.
Q: What were you in a previous life?
A: A crutch, to lean on.
Q: Why be moral?
A: An orange Beetle with punctured tyres.

iv.

When Breton published 'Souvenir du Mexique' in *Minotaure*, the first image he used was Álvarez Bravo's *Striking Worker, Assassinated*. There was no planning, no thought, no stagecraft, no sketches: this was pure automatism. The fluids of death sprawling out from a face graced with the flush of youth. The open eyes and wet hair. The Mexican flag in close background. Death perceived by the living, an image unmatched until Graciela Iturbide chanced upon that man near Pachuca.

And he would be called Mr Death.

Q: When will pain subside?
A: The purple jacarandas line an urban walkway.

Jagua, Cienfuegos Bay

In a pool of shallow seawater a turtle rests on a bed of rusting coins. Squat castle protects the bay from those English pirates. Stone on stone by dragged-in slaves from Trinidad. The Lady in Blue still haunts the moat and dungeon. We emerge from the darkness of karabiners and cutlasses and a scale model of the bilateral twin reactor plant that sits still like a mosque on the horizon spied from the boat where we stood at the stern beside a man cradling an ancient television in his arms like a newborn. The government graffiti on the seawall: *Bienvenidos Socialista*. From the turret I see the abandoned rectangles of the Soviets, hundreds held on from the nineties, still rejecting Perestroika, staying put, hoping, existing somehow in an empty nuclear city. Bored horses and cans of sun-boiled beer blaze. The Caribbean heat is amoral. Smoke from a lizard corpse and my own skin bubbling before my eyes drives us to the restaurant. Meaty lobster tail split and grilled with a fillet of wreckfish, a mussel shell filled with cold octopus, diced with herbs, seven-year-old rum and my face in a bucket of ice. A pelican statue, red kerchief round its beak, stands watch over the bay. From the boat back to Cienfuegos, the sugar refinery's stripy chimney reminds us of Dublin and our eyes down to *ooh* at the aquatic propulsion of jelly, each bell inflating mechanically and expelling renewable water from its organism, an entire world blue and gelatinous with a million medusas, one of our planet's oldest creatures, her most energy-efficient children, the locomotion of pulsating umbrellas, all of them, like us, dashing somewhere else because they have to, because they can.

Icnocuicatl

versions of anonymous Nahuatl grief songs

i.

i'm drinking mushroom pulque
i'm wretched in this country
i enjoy nothing
utterly helpless in this land

i look upon death with disgust
but what's there to be done
                    nothing, really

you're all just depraved, fashioning something

even if it's true
even if we really are united like the feathers
of a quetzal headdress
even if we really are all stones of the same necklace
none of this is real

you're all depraved, fashioning something, depraved

my friend, my friend
maybe my true friend
we respect each other
but we both must perish
here are your flowers
take them

ii.

is there really anything real
only the flowers are wanted
desired

there is flowery death
and there is joyful death

my little heart be brave
nobody here will live

iii.

god makes fun of us
all just chasing a dream

ah, my friends
our hearts entrust
when moved we rejoice

verdure and paint

he makes us live
knows and decides
how all men will die

but
                      nobody
                      nobody
                      nobody
really lives on this earth

iv.

alone on the earth with our sadness

he hides us in a chest, a casket, our god
                    enshrouds his own people

perhaps i'll be able to think down there
able to see the face of my mother
                    the face of my father
maybe lent a few songs, a few words

ah, but no
everything is wrong—he just left us here

El Indio Triste, *a Lament*

Human to legend, statue to ghost
crouched and mumbling
mocked and buffeted
—the excruciating
music of what's happened

At once he sees:

poxed cadavers dismembered, pushed down the canal to the
drinking water of bearded degenerates, diseased blood mixed
into their bread. The departed, mythological jostle with the
now. Copycat genuflections, makeshift crucifixes, the early
cargo cult of New World Catholicism. Plastic *fayuca* that will
float on seawater. A transgender giant(ess) fashioned from
bronze. Candles. Superimposed negatives from the hillsides,
far from the lakeshore, a swirling fairy wind of rubbish over
Santa Fe, the business district built on a dump. He sees the
Wexfordian astrologist burned at the stake. A half-moon with
a grin. A wine-coloured flag in a puddle. A rain of stars and
gods, then a pale wash of a mango watercolour for the early
risers, the sun dribbling over the rooftops. (Nine hundred Latin
psalms couldn't stop the flames.) He sees the post-earthquake
slant of colonial chapels, naked protestors at the statue of
Cuauhtémoc, a pillar of skulls only partially excavated.
Muscovado in a quicksand of whipped egg whites. Dust. The
formation of dust. Inhaled. Foil wrappers and cigarette butts.
The summer pathways rippling. The short-term blossoming of
the jacarandas in spring. Sweat, grime, a multitude of climates
simultaneously glimpsed, a mandarin petroleum.

*

Of course, the sad Indian story may be apocryphal. A defeated *cacique* held onto his fortunes in exchange for his collaboration. One night he failed to warn the Spaniards of a planned uprising, having devoted too much time to alcohol, food, sins of the flesh. All his possessions were confiscated. Dejected, he would be seen crouched and sobbing, destitute on the street corner. After he died, a statue replaced him. A reminder of what happens.

From 1869 to 1928, *Calle del Correo Mayor* was named *Calle del Indio Triste*. Both names still marked by plaques. Above them a stone relief of a half-moon with a large eye, a mouth and a nose, stares down to the corner where the sad Indian squatted in his penury.

*

He sees the lovers of Tlatelolco, their touching fingerbones. He sees the effects of cholera on the watery capital, a flimsy lid like a slab on the lake. He sees Don Carlos, son of Nezahualpilli, burnt alive for attempting to bring back the old religion and he understands. The canals filled in, then the streets flooded, he sees a man fall, get trapped by a vehicle and drown on a thoroughfare in the middle of the day. The snakes of the underground. Coconut, shredded and cradled in a candied lime skin. He sees intestines spilled into the dust, groped for and then put back in.

Glyphic codex under Latinate script.
The seepage still so evident, the bleeding into, so fresh.
                              This entire city a palimpsest.

My feet are open sores
Two black suns
burn in my face
You do not wish to know me

The statue either crumbled
was moved or dismantled

and my raw lips pulse
like edges of a wound

Now the wash of dawn
caramelizes, it hardens
—progression to a treacle evening
the sweetness of decay
the insects, the rats
the ending of day

A rotating cast of tableaux vivants
has taken his place and the music
of what happens still happens

El Fuerte, Sinaloa

Felipa says that crickets always make noise, never even stopping to catch their breath, in order to drown out the cries of the souls that suffer in Purgatory. The day the crickets die the world will be filled with the screams of holy souls …

—Juan Rulfo, *El Llano en llamas*

i. Aubade

A brief limbo. The train approaches, rattling inland from Los Mochis. Time to kill before boarding. An entire town submerged in the pink translucence of grapefruit juice. A desire to record this colonial outpost. To compose a block of prose as robust, squat and rectangular as the fortress that names this settlement. A desire that falters as the naming of things poses problems.

'I kill men down by the water.'

I photograph the fortress with those dawn-lit flowers in the foreground. *Bugambilias*, I know what they are, in Spanish, at least. Every poet here does. Their petals a magenta paper crunching on the laneways from here to Chetumal. A thorny ornamental that explodes against stone, volcanic or otherwise. But this flower, though pink, is something else. I sneak behind the structure to a quiet vista of a meandering waterway, a panorama that I pocket unthinkingly. The grating of insect legs filled the night but the silence now of morning is startling. I am the only one around.

The sun low and blinding. The moment has stretched. I run back to the hotel to find Lily waiting with a taxi. Quick and dusty we make our way to the station. The driver tells me that the pink flower is, in fact, a *rosa laurel*. Commonly used to adorn traffic islands in Sinaloa. It's poisonous, deadly. Nerium oleander: 'Neros', water. 'Ollyo', I kill. 'Aner', man.

'I kill men down by the water.'

ii. Nocturne

On the boardwalk Lily dampens softly the riverside air, sobbing into my chest her fears of not mothering. Her thighs. One scarred. The other tattooed:

Three peonies, one for each	unopened
A white butterfly	*Dealán Dé*
A fourth one opened	a hopeful shade of grey

We cling to each other besieged on all sides by the encompassing clitter of the nocturnal. The insects feasting loudly upon the carcass of the night. We surrender to its darkness, the hypnosis of the stridulating crickets. I think I see the dark twinkle of an alligator drifting by but it must have been a paddling of ducks or scraps of plastic. Closer still. Everything but ourselves a moat.

Notes

'And What Is My Heart'
'And What Is My Heart' is a reworking of Kuno Meyer's rendition of the anonymous Irish poem 'The Mothers' Lament at the Slaughter of the Innocents'.

'Kingfisher Haibun' etc.
'Kingfisher Haibun', 'What the Swan Can Teach Us', 'Hy Brasil', 'Of an Island Where Corpses Exposed to the Elements Do Not Suffer Decay', 'Things You Can Do With a Grasshopper' and 'First Snake in Ireland' incorporate elements of Gerald of Wales's *Topographia Hibernica*.

'*After the Storm*'
'*After the Storm*' is an ekphrastic poem inspired by *Después de la tormenta*, a 1910 painting by Diego Rivera.

'*The Dead*' etc.
Every word in the poems titled '*The Dead*' are taken from the James Joyce story of the same name. The following poems also use vocabulary gleaned only from specific Joyce stories: 'Towards a Decision' (from 'A Little Cloud'); 'Traitor' (from 'A Painful Case'); 'The Dream Before' (from 'Two Gallants'); and 'I Crammed My Mouth' (from 'The Sisters'). All from the short story collection *Dubliners*, 1914.

'Cocoon'
'Cocoon' incorporates the entirety of Giuseppe Ungaretti's short poem 'Mattina' (from *L'Allegria*, 1931) and contains phrases borrowed from Seamus Heaney (from the translation of *The Burial at Thebes*, 2004) and Kurt Vonnegut (from

the book *Mother Night*, 1962). Latin phrases are from the 'Dies irae' included in the Roman Missal Requiem Mass.

'Notes on Black Vultures'
This poem contains a quotation from S. Thomas, J. Eric's article 'Pictorial Synonyms and Homonyms in the Maya Dresden Codex', 1963.

'Dublin Nocturne'
'Dublin Nocturne' contains phrases borrowed from Tom Waits (from the songs 'Nighthawk Postcards' and 'Putnam County', 1975) and James Joyce (from the novel *Finnegans Wake*, 1939).

'Tamaulipas Amergin'
'Tamaulipas Amergin' is inspired by the Song of Amergin which legend suggests may be the earliest poem to be composed in the Irish language. The *'Tamaulipas Amergin'* sequence brings together elements of anonymous Irish nature poetry (taken from *The Book of Irish Verse: Irish Poetry from the Sixth Century to the Present*, edited by John Montague, 1976) and the story of the *Batallón de San Patricio*, a small group of mostly Irish soldiers who, having switched sides, fought for Mexico against invading U.S. forces in the mid-nineteenth century. 'Mammy / *Nonantzin*' is a translation of an anonymous Nahuatl lyric often mistakenly attributed to Nezahualcóyotl.

'Icnocuicatl'
These poems are versions of anonymous Nahuatl lyrics found in *La tinta negra y roja, Antología de la poesía náhuatl*, edited by Miguel León-Portilla, 2012.

'*El Indio Triste*, a Lament'
Italicized words on page 90 are taken from *The Poems of Sweeny Peregrine*, 1976 by Trevor Joyce. 'The music of what happens' is a phrase taken from the 'The Finest Music' section of the Fenian Cycle as translated by James Stephens in *The Finest Music, An Anthology of Early Irish Lyrics*, edited by Maurice Riordan, 2014.

'El Fuerte, Sinaloa'
The epigraph by Juan Rulfo is from the short story collection *El Llano en llamas*, 1953.

Acknowledgements

My thanks to the editors of the following journals and anthologies in which some of these poems have previously appeared, often in different versions: *Abridged, Banshee, Catalyst, Channel, The Cormorant, Crannóg, The Honest Ulsterman, The Penny Dreadful, The Pickled Body, Poetry Ireland Review, Poets for Ayotzinapa, Romance Options, Smithereens Literary Magazine, Southword, SPROUT* and *The Stinging Fly*. 'Botany' was commissioned for the inaugural edition of *SPROUT*, an eco-urban poetry journal. Many thanks to Jonathan Brennan for collaborating on a short film version of 'Four Attempts at Making a Human'. The film has been screened at festivals in Mexico City, Cork, and Drumshanbo (where it won the inaugural Drumshanbo Written Word Weekend Poetry Film Competition).

I am extremely grateful to the Banshees for taking a chance on me and agreeing to publish this work. Laura, Claire and Eimear, thank you *so* much for your belief and enthusiasm. Jessica Traynor worked as editor on this collection and her suggestions were insightful and cogent. Simply put, she understood the book and made it better. Thanks Jess.

Many thanks to Eiléan Ní Chuilleanáin for nominating me as recipient of the 2018 Ireland Chair of Poetry bursary, thanks also to the Ireland Chair of Poetry Trust.

I am very grateful to Culture Ireland and the Embassy of Ireland in Mexico for assistance in travelling to poetry festivals in Colombia, Nicaragua and the US in recent years.

Thanks to Magda Bogin and everyone at Under the Volcano: Paul Muldoon, Devi Laskar, Kristina Bicher, Annabella Eatherley and Deborah Casillas.

Special thanks to Dimitra Xidous and Sarah Byrne for encouraging words when I most needed them and to Tim MacGabhann, Keith Payne, Cal Doyle, Cody Copeland, Grant Cogswell and Philip Coleman who read versions or excerpts of this manuscript and offered advice and/or encouragement along the way: I am in your debt.

Finally, thanks to my family and friends. To Lily, my first reader and to Finn, my youngest: there would be no poems without you.